Understanding Macroeconomics
with
Gods of Money

John Crews

Text copyright © 2016 John Crews

All Rights Reserved

ISBN 978-1537107998

Table of Contents

Foreword v
1. Introduction to *Gods of Money* 1
   ABOUT GODS OF MONEY 1
   THE ENVIRONMENT 2
      VIEWPORT 3
      DASHBOARD 7
      CONTROL PANEL 10
   STARTING AND RUNNING GODS OF MONEY 13
2. Gross Domestic Product 17
3. Personal Income 21
4. Taxes & Revenue 23
5. Budget & Expenditures 25
6. Deficit & Debt 29
7. Federal Reserve 31
8. Gold Standard 35
9. Employment Tools 37
10. Active Mode 39
Appendix I: Recommended Reading 43
Appendix II. Economic Data Resources 45
Index 47

Foreword

This book is designed to be a companion to the *Gods of Money* app. *Gods of Money* is the first app for visualizing and simulating the U.S. economy. It shows how the Federal Reserve, Congress, and the White House manipulate the creation and flow of money across the nation.

This volume is intended to assist the reader in using *Gods of Money* to learn the basics of macroeconomics. It affords a suitable platform for more thorough explanations of the features and uses of the app. The reader is guided, chapter by chapter, from an introduction to the app, through visualization of the major parts of the U.S. economy, to instructions on how to use "active mode" to experiment with manipulating the economy. Finally, two appendices list recommended further reading and links to macroeconomics resources.

More information about the app, questions, and comments are welcome at godsofmoney.com.

1. Introduction to *Gods of Money*

ABOUT *GODS OF MONEY*

Gods of Money is an iPad app for learning the basics of macroeconomics.

Macroeconomics

Macroeconomics is the part of economics concerned with large-scale or general economic factors, such as interest rates and national productivity. Macroeconomics is important because it tells us how well the citizens of the U.S. are doing financially. When the U.S. economy grows the people usually receive a higher standard of living.

With a basic knowledge of macroeconomics, individuals can make better personal financial decisions, such as when to buy a house or a new car. People can also make better-informed decisions about whom to vote for when electing presidents and members of congress.

The Gods of Money App

With *Gods of Money* you can see:
- How the government manipulates the flow of money across the country
- How much money is made by businesses
- Where the government gets its money and how it is spent
- How much money goes to individual households
- How the Federal Reserve System, Congress, and the White House create and manipulate the U.S. money supply and understand why they are called the "Gods of Money."

Gods of Money provides a unique educational experience on how the United States economy works through visualization and participation.

Watch or Participate
You can view how the U.S. economy has grown and changed over time. Or, you can use Active mode and try your hand at manipulating the economy by playing the roles of the Federal Reserve System, the White House, and Congress - the "Gods of Money."

Your Grade
After running *Gods of Money* in Active mode for at least one year, your performance is evaluated and you receive a letter grade. Your grade is based on several factors which indicate the change in the standard of living for U.S. citizens. A grade of C+ or higher means that most people are better off, and a score less than C means the standard of living declined or improved more slowly than the historical average. You'll get a large penalty if the economy collapses, and a big bonus if the economy excels.

The Gods of Money Guide
The *Gods of Money* Guide provides information on important economic issues as they arise. The Guide's pop-up windows tell why an issue is important, what actions to take (if any), and more detailed information if requested. The Guide can be turned on or off under Settings.

THE ENVIRONMENT
The *Gods of Money* environment is divided into 4 main parts:
- Viewport
- News crawl
- Dashboard
- Control panel

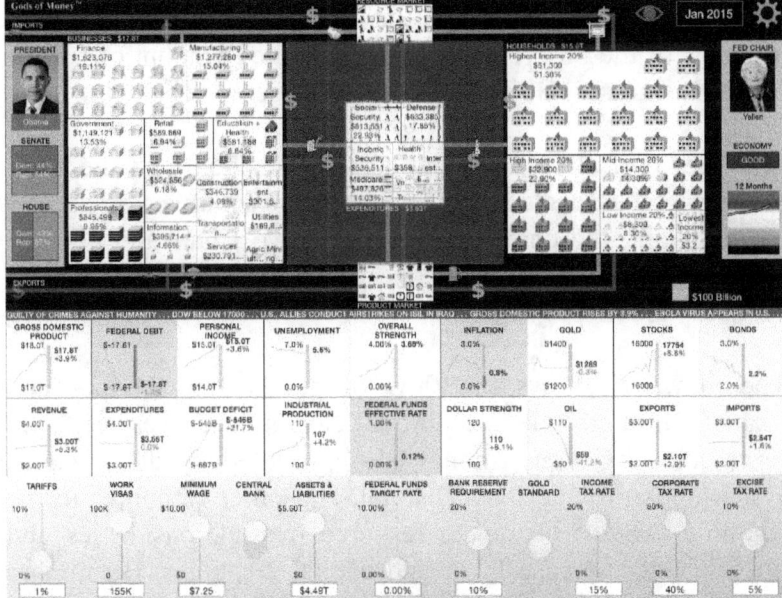

Figure 1. The main interface

VIEWPORT

The Viewport shows money and goods flowing through the economy as a diagram. The relative sizes of businesses, the U.S. government, and household income are displayed.

The Viewport also displays the current game date near the upper right corner. Tap the date to pause the game; tap again to resume.

The Settings button appears as a "gear" icon in the upper right. Tap the "gear" icon to access the settings menu or to quit the current game. The settings menu is used to change the:
- Display
- Sound
- Speed
- Guide

When in Watch mode an "eye" icon appears left of the date. Tap the "eye" icon to change to Active mode.

The Money Scale appears in the lower right of the Viewport. The size of the box represents the indicated amount of money in the Businesses, Government, and Households boxes.

The Viewport also shows the current president and the party makeup of the Senate and House of Representatives on the left. On the right, the current Federal Reserve Chair and a graph showing the current and one-year status of the overall economy are displayed.

The viewport shows the flow of goods and services and money through the economy. Goods and services are represented by icons; money is represented by dollar signs. Households provide labor, capital, and other resources to the resource market. From the resource market, businesses and government purchase labor and capital resources. Businesses provide their goods and services to the product market, where individuals and government buy things. The government collects taxes from and provides services to businesses and households. You also see money "flying" from government to businesses and households. This represents government payments such as Social Security, welfare, and Medicare. When the economy is doing well, the flow goes faster; when the economy is doing poorly, the flow goes slower.

Sounds
The app also includes background sounds. When the economy is doing okay, you will hear the sounds of construction, factories running, and busy offices. When the economy is doing very well, you will hear the sounds of restaurants and parties. When the economy is doing worse, you may hear wind howling and dogs barking. To turn sound on or off, tap the "gear" icon in the upper right, then tap **Settings**.

News Crawl
The News Crawl under the Viewport gives information on how the economy is doing. When in Active mode, keep an eye on the news to get feedback on how you are doing. In Watch mode the News also displays historical headlines at a rate of about one per month.

Dashboard
The Dashboard shows gauges of various economic indicators. See more details below.

Control Panel
The Control Panel provides the tools that you can use to influence the economy. See more details below.

BUSINESSES
The size of the Businesses box is determined by the annual Gross Domestic Product (GDP), the total of all goods and services produced in the country in one year. GDP is covered in more detail in Chapter 2. Double-tap on Businesses to zoom in.

The business sectors are:
- Finance, insurance, real estate, rental, and leasing
- Manufacturing
- Professional and business services
- Educational services, health care, and social assistance
- Wholesale trade
- Retail trade
- Information
- Arts, entertainment, recreation, accommodation, and food services
- Construction
- Transportation and warehousing
- Mining
- Government
- Other services, except government
- Utilities
- Agriculture, forestry, fishing, and hunting

GOVERNMENT EXPENSES
The size of the Government box is determined by the annual outlays as indicated by the federal budget or by revenue generated by taxes and other means. The outlays are organized by function. The functions are:
- Social Security

- National Defense
- Income Security
- Medicare
- Health (Medicaid)
- Net Interest
- Veterans Benefits and Services
- Transportation
- Education Training, Employment and Social Services
- Administration of Justice
- International Affairs
- Natural Resources and Environment
- Community and Regional Development
- Agriculture
- General Science, Space, and Technology
- General Government
- Energy

Once per year (in January) you can alter the budget. Many functions have a mandatory minimum amount that must be spent. Specifying amounts less than the mandatory amount would be very difficult and politically unpopular.

Failure to pay the mandatory minimum for the net interest on the national debt would mean that the U.S. would default on its financial obligations, leading to economic calamity in the U.S. and around the world. Expenditures is covered in more detail in Chapter 5.

Tap to switch to Government Revenue. Double-tap to zoom in.

GOVERNMENT REVENUE
The U.S. government raises revenue by collecting taxes and fees and sometimes by selling assets. The categories of revenue are:
- Individual income tax
- Corporate income tax
- Social insurance and retirement taxes
- Excise tax
- Other

Government revenue is covered in more detail in Chapter 4.

Tap to switch to Government Expenses. Double-tap to zoom in.

HOUSEHOLDS
The size of the Households box is determined by the annual total household income. Households are divided into 5 groups. Each group contains 20% of all households sorted by income. The size of each group reflects its annual income. The dollar figure is the average household income for the group. Personal income is covered in more detail in Chapter 3. Double-tap to zoom in.

RESOURCE MARKET
The Resource Market is where resources are exchanged for money. Resources include:
- Labor
- Land
- Capital
- Entrepreneurial Ability

Households receive money in the form of wages, rents, interest, profits, etc.

PRODUCT MARKET
The Product Market is where goods and services are exchanged for money. Some goods and services are:
- Houses, cars, electronics
- Clothes, food, medicine
- Finance, health care, shipping

DASHBOARD
The dashboard panel shows the value of various economic indicators. Indicator values are updated once per month. Many indicators show the percentage change over one year.

Gross Domestic Product
Gross Domestic Product or GDP is the sum of all goods and services produced in the country in one year. Since the end of World War II, GDP has grown at an average rate of 6.64% per year. The size of the Businesses box corresponds to the GDP.

Federal Debt
The U.S. federal government debt is the amount owed by the U.S. government due to its borrowing to pay its expenses. It is theoretically possible to have a federal surplus if the debt were completely paid off and revenue exceeded expenses. The size of the Federal Debt (or Federal Surplus) box corresponds to this value.

Personal Income
Personal income is the total income for all households per year. The size of the Households box corresponds to Personal Income.

Unemployment
The rate of unemployment is the percentage of working-age people who are available and looking for work. This does not include people who are part-time or underemployed. Since World War II, the unemployment rate has averaged 5.8%.

Revenue
Revenue is the total income for the U.S. government per year. Tax rates and other factors affect revenue.

Expenditures
Expenditures is the total amount of money spent by the U.S. government for the year. Setting the budget controls total expenditures.

Budget Deficit/Budget Surplus
The budget deficit (or surplus) is the difference between all federal receipts and expenditures. When expenditures exceed revenue, a shortfall or deficit occurs, and the federal debt increases. When revenue exceeds expenditures, a surplus occurs and the federal debt decreases.

Industrial Production
Industrial production is shown as an index and indicates the output for all manufacturing, mining, and utilities in the U.S. The industrial production index value was 100 in 2007.

Overall Strength
The overall strength or weakness of the economy is displayed in the Overall Strength indicator. A positive value means that the average citizen is better off, while a negative value means harder times for the U.S.

Federal Funds Effective Rate
The federal funds effective rate is the interest rate at which federal funds trade. It is an important benchmark in financial markets and influences the interest rates consumers pay for loans and receive in interest on savings. A high interest rate slows the economy by discouraging lending. A low interest rate may improve the economy by encouraging lending but it discourages saving money and may lead to high inflation. Since 1954 the federal funds effective rate has averaged 5.1%.

Inflation
Inflation is the sustained increase in the general prices of goods and services over a period of time. High rates of inflation can lead to consumer hoarding and social unrest. A very high rate of inflation, called hyperinflation, can lead to great disruptions in the economy. Historically, inflation has averaged about 3.9% per year.

Gold
The Gold indicator shows the spot price for 1 troy ounce of fine gold. The price of gold is influenced by commercial and industrial demand, and is often seen as a safe haven in times of economic upheaval.

Stocks
The Stocks indicator shows the Dow Jones Industrial Average. Stocks generally rise with a growing economy. However, stocks rising quickly may indicate a bubble which can burst, sending prices rapidly downward.

Bonds
The Bonds indicator shows the yield of the 10-year Treasury note. The yield is the return that is received for a bond. The primary influence on bond yields is the interest rate.

Dollar Strength
The Dollar Strength indicator shows the Real Narrow Effective Exchange Rate for United States index. The index was 100 in 2010. A higher value indicates a stronger dollar which means that U.S. money has more value compared with the money of other countries. However, a strong dollar makes U.S. goods more expensive in other countries and hurts companies that sell their goods outside the U.S.

Oil
The Oil indicator shows the price of West Texas Intermediate Crude, which is a good indication of overall energy prices. Higher oil prices may indicate higher energy demand and a growing economy. But if the price is too high the economy may slow.

Exports
The Exports indicator shows the total amount of goods and services exported out of the U.S. to other countries.

Imports
The Imports indicator shows the total spent on goods and services brought into the U.S. from other countries.

CONTROL PANEL
The Control panel provides access to the tools used to manipulate the amount and flow of money. In Watch mode, you can see how the controls were changed and how the economy was affected. In Active mode, you can have your turn at manipulating the amount of money and how it moves throughout the economy.

Tariffs
A tariff is a tax on imported goods or services. Tariffs are used to raise revenue or protect domestic industries from foreign competition. Tariffs raise prices for consumers and may lead to trade wars.

Work Visas
Workers from foreign countries need visas to work in the U.S. This value represents the annual number of H-1B work visas which are for jobs that require a college degree. Raising the number of visas allowed per year may increase domestic production, but is politically unpopular because it is seen as giving American jobs to foreign nationals.

Minimum Wage
Minimum wage is the lowest amount that an employer can pay a worker for one hour of labor. Designed to prevent exploitation of workers, most economists believe a minimum wage makes production less efficient and increases unemployment. The minimum wage varies greatly from country to country: as of 2011, in Australia the minimum wage was $15.75; in the U.S, $7.25; in Mexico, $0.58. Some countries such as Switzerland have no minimum wage.

Central Bank
The U.S. central bank, the Federal Reserve or the "Fed," can be turned off, imitating the conditions that would exist if the Fed were decommissioned. With the Fed turned off, interest rates float and no securities are held. The Fed sets the minimum bank reserve requirements, but in the absence of the Fed, it is assumed that another agency or Congress would assume that task. The Fed balance sheet, controlled by the Assets and Liabilities control, must be 0 before the Central Bank can be turned off.

Assets & Liabilities
In addition to setting the interest rate, the Federal Reserve also manipulates the money supply by purchasing and selling financial securities, growing and shrinking its balance sheet. Increasing the money supply may lead to higher growth, but could also bring higher inflation.

Federal Funds Target Rate
The primary tool of the Federal Reserve is the ability to set the interest rate. When the economy is growing slowly or even shrinking, a low interest rate can spur growth. However, when

an interest rate is too low for too long it may create high inflation. If inflation is determined to be too high, a higher interest rate will slow the economy.

Bank Reserve Requirement
Banks are required to keep a percentage of their assets in reserve in case many depositors withdraw their money at once. A low bank reserve requirement frees up money and spurs the economy, but it also risks causing banks to close. A high bank reserve requirement can slow down a fast-growing economy.

Gold Standard
A commodity standard is a monetary system in which the country's currency is based on fixed amounts of a stable commodity, usually gold. A "gold standard" keeps inflation low in the long term but requires a country to keep large amounts of gold reserves. The gold standard was used in the U.S. for many years, but was abandoned in 1971.

If a commodity standard is not used, the country has "fiat money;" currency that is declared legal tender but is not backed by a physical commodity. Almost all countries use fiat money today. Fiat money runs the risk of becoming worthless due to hyperinflation.

Income Tax Rate
The Income Tax Rate control sets the rate paid by the median taxpayer. The government gets the majority of its revenue from personal income tax.

Corporate Tax Rate
The Corporate Tax Rate control sets the maximum rate paid by corporations. About 10% of federal government receipts come from corporate income taxes. If the corporate tax rate is too low, the U.S. loses potential income; if it is too high, corporations will move to countries where the corporate tax rate is lower. The actual tax collected is less than the maximum income tax rate due to exemptions.

Excise Tax Rate

Excise taxes are charged on the manufacturer or wholesaler of certain goods, including alcohol, tobacco products, ammunition, and gasoline. Increasing excise taxes would generate additional revenue but it could lower GDP and could be politically unpopular. The Excise Tax Rate control sets the rate relative to 10 times GDP.

STARTING AND RUNNING *GODS OF MONEY*

Launch the app on your device by one of these methods:
- Tap the *Gods of Money* app icon.
- Search for *Gods of Money*:
    o Tap the Home button.
    o From the middle of the screen, swipe down.
    o Enter "*Gods of Money*" in the search bar.
    o Under Top Hits, tap *Gods of Money*.
- Open Siri, then say "Start *Gods of Money*."
- In a classroom, the instructor may launch the app for you.

The first time the app is run, you will see a window informing you that you must agree to the terms and conditions before proceeding. Tap **Read Terms** to read the terms. Tap **Agree** to accept the terms and conditions.

When the main menu appears, you will see three buttons:
- **Start** starts a new session
- **Learn** displays the instructions
- **View** displays the highest recorded grades

Tap **Start**. The start menu appears. On this menu you can choose to start a new simulation in active mode or view historical data in watch mode. Tap **Watch** or **Start**.

On the next menu select a start date. If starting a new simulation, also specify the end date:
- 1 Year
- 2 Years
- 5 Years
- 10 Years

- No End Date

Tap **Start**. After a few moments, the session will begin. The budget window will be displayed. The budget window will automatically dismiss after 30 seconds of inactivity. Or, you can dismiss the window by tapping the checkmark in the upper right corner.

After a few months of game time, a *Gods of Money* Guide window will appear. The window lists an economic issue that may need attention. Tap the blue arrow on the left to expand the guide. The window will expand with 3 tabs:
- **Importance** describes the importance of the issue presented
- **Actions** suggests what actions are often taken to address the issue
- **More** gives more detail about the issue

Tap the checkmark in the upper right corner to dismiss the window. Tap the X in the lower right corner to turn off the Guide. The Guide can be turned on and off under Settings.

As the app runs, you will see various tip windows appear. The tips provide information to help you run and use *Gods of Money*. On each tip window you can tap **Remind me later** and the tip will appear again in the future. Tap **Got it** after you have learned the tip. Tips inform you how to pause the app; how to pause the budget window; how to change from government expenditures to revenue; how to zoom in on Businesses, Households, and Government; etc.

In Watch mode the session will run until the end of the available data. In Active mode the session will run until the specified end date. If no end date was specified, the session will run indefinitely. However, an Active mode session will end if the economy collapses or it becomes self-sustaining (see Chapter 10). To stop a session early, tap the settings "gear" icon in the upper right of the viewport, then tap **Quit**.

If the session has run for one year or more, you will receive a letter grade from A+ to D- or F. The grade is based on the performance of the economy during the session. A grade of C means that the standard of living is about the same throughout the session. A higher grade means the economy did better, and people enjoyed a higher standard of living, while a lower grade means the standard of living declined. If the economy collapsed completely, you will see a grade of F for failure.

If you achieve one of the 10 best grades, you will be invited to enter a name for your economy for the high grades list and the High Grades window will be displayed. To erase all high grades, tap the bottom left of the High Grades window. Clearing the high grades cannot be undone. To dismiss the High Grades window, tap the checkmark in the upper right. After dismissal, the main menu will appear.

2. Gross Domestic Product

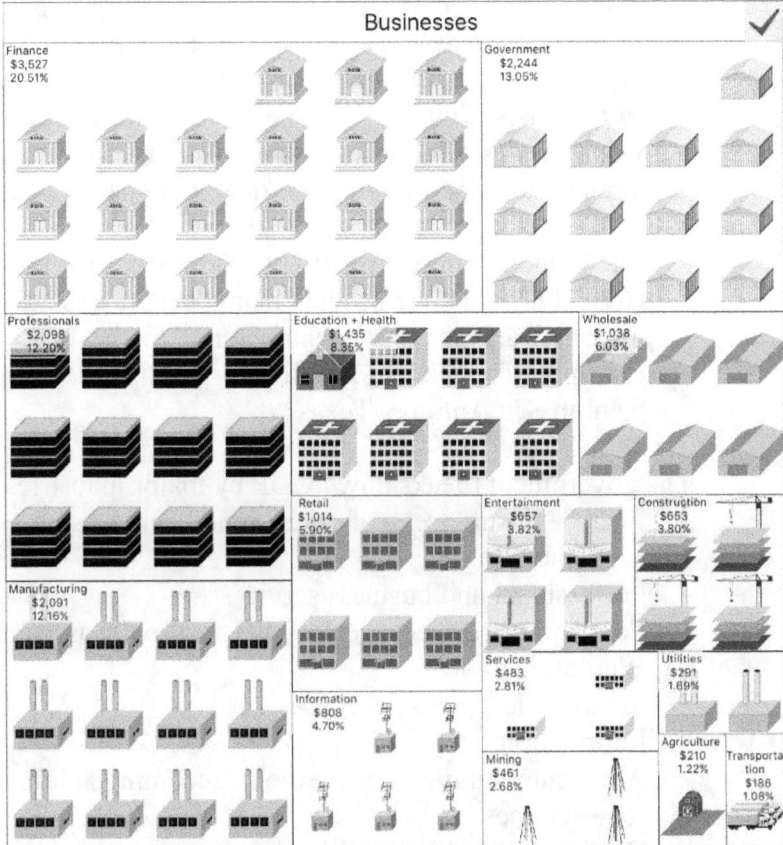

Figure 2. The Businesses window shows GDP by industry

The "Gross Domestic Product" is the sum of all goods and services produced in the country in one year.
- "Gross" refers to the total amount, before any deductions.
- "Domestic" means within the borders of the U.S.
- "Product" refers to the value of all the things made and services provided.

"Gross Domestic Product" is abbreviated "GDP." It is calculated and reported 4 times per year by the U.S. government. Every country has its own GDP.

What are some examples of products and services that contribute to GDP? Only things that are produced in the U.S. are part of GDP.
- Almost all smart phones and tablets are not manufactured in the U.S., so they are not included in the GDP of the U.S.
- But transporting the phone from the dock to a wholesaler, storing it in a warehouse, transporting it to a retail store, and retail store operations are all part of GDP.
- The manufacture of imported goods is not included in GDP, but some items that many people assume are imported are actually manufactured in the U.S. One example: Toyota builds full-size pickup trucks at its plant in San Antonio, Texas.

The government breaks down GDP by major industries:
- Finance, insurance, real estate, rental, and leasing
- Manufacturing
- Professional and business services
- Educational services, health care, and social assistance
- Wholesale trade
- Retail trade
- Information
- Arts, entertainment, recreation, accommodation, and food services
- Construction
- Transportation and warehousing
- Mining, including petroleum
- Government
- Other services, except government
- Utilities
- Agriculture, forestry, fishing, and hunting

GDP is often used as an indicator of living standards. When real GDP increases, the standard of living (usually) increases as well.
- "Standard of Living" is the general level of wealth and comfort experienced by people.

- A stagnant or falling GDP is bad because it means the standard of living will fall.
- When GDP decreases for 6 months or more, the economy is said to be in a recession.
- A "Recession" is a general slowdown in economic activity: people make less money, so they spend less money, so businesses make less money, and more people lose their jobs.

3. Personal Income

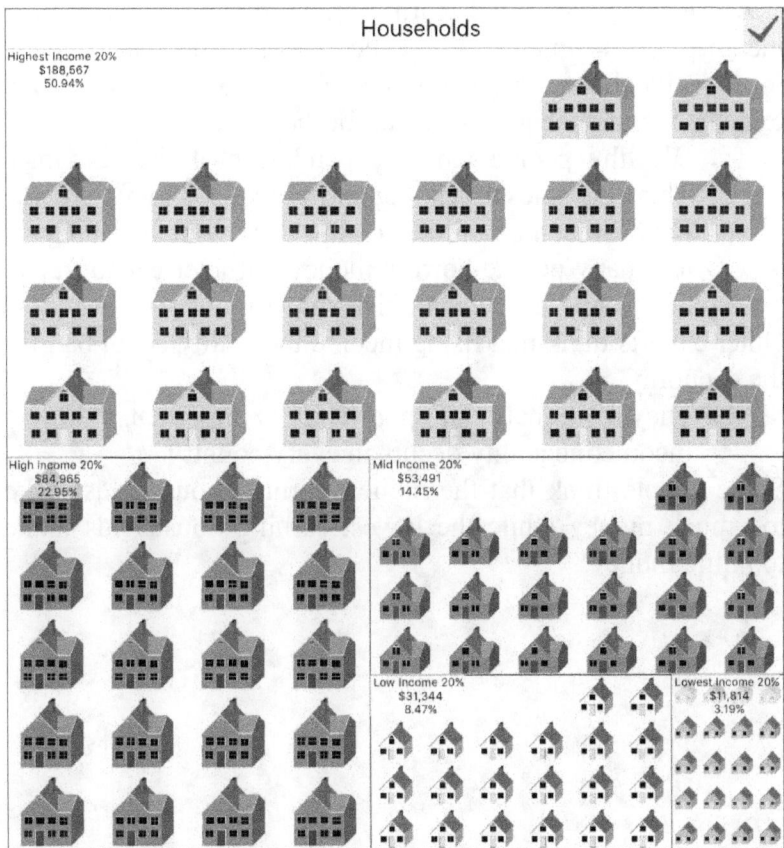

Figure 3. The Households window shows personal income by quintile

"Personal Income" is the sum of all income received by private households in the country in one year. A household may be one person, a family, or several generations living under one roof.

The Households window displays personal income. The window is divided into 5 parts, or quintiles. Each quintile represents 20% of all households in the country; that is, each quintile represents the same number of people. The size of each quintile represents the average income for each quintile. In 2015, the quintile representing the highest income made

50.94% of all personal income. The quintile representing the lowest income made 3.19% of all personal income.

Because some households earn more money than others, their incomes are unequal: this is called income inequality. Some income inequality is inevitable. Some experts think that extreme income inequality is bad for the economy.
- Wealthy people tend to spend less of their savings. This causes less spending and slower economic growth.
- Lower-income families tend to borrow more money. If too many people borrow money but later cannot repay their loans, a financial crisis may follow.

Other experts think that rising income inequality is not bad for the economy.
- They say equality of opportunity is important.
- Income inequality occurs in every country.

Some people think that the highest earning households make too much money while the lowest earning households make too little money.

4. Taxes & Revenue

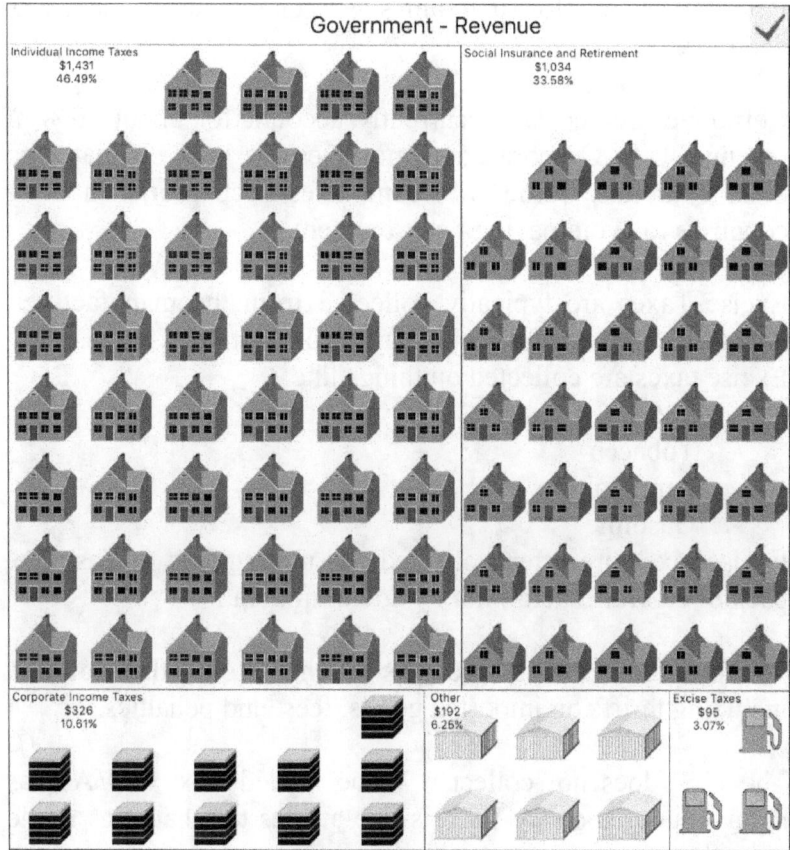

Figure 4. The Revenue window

The U.S. government raises money primarily by assessing taxes. The main taxes are:
- Personal income taxes
- Social Insurance and Retirement taxes, often called "Payroll" taxes
- Corporate income taxes
- Excise taxes

The U.S. government gets most of its revenue from personal income taxes. Most personal income tax revenue comes from taxes on wages and salaries. Sources of passive income, such as interest, dividends, rental property income, etc., are usually taxed at a lower rate.

Payroll taxes pay for such things as Social Security, Medicare, and more.

Corporate income taxes currently account for about 10% of revenue. U.S. Corporate income taxes are high compared to other countries. Some U.S. companies keep profits in other countries to avoid paying taxes on them.

Excise Taxes are typically collected from the manufacturer, not at the point of sale, so the buyer does not "see" them.
Excise taxes are collected on things like
- Alcohol
- Tobacco
- Ammunition
- Gasoline

Excise taxes are often collected per unit (gallon of gasoline, pack of cigarettes, etc.) not by dollar amount.

The U.S. government also gets revenue from other sources, including tariffs on imported goods, fees, and penalties.

The U.S. does not collect a Value Added Tax, or VAT, as many countries do. A VAT is like a sales tax that goes to the federal government.

The Whitehouse and Congress set the federal tax rates.

5. Budget & Expenditures

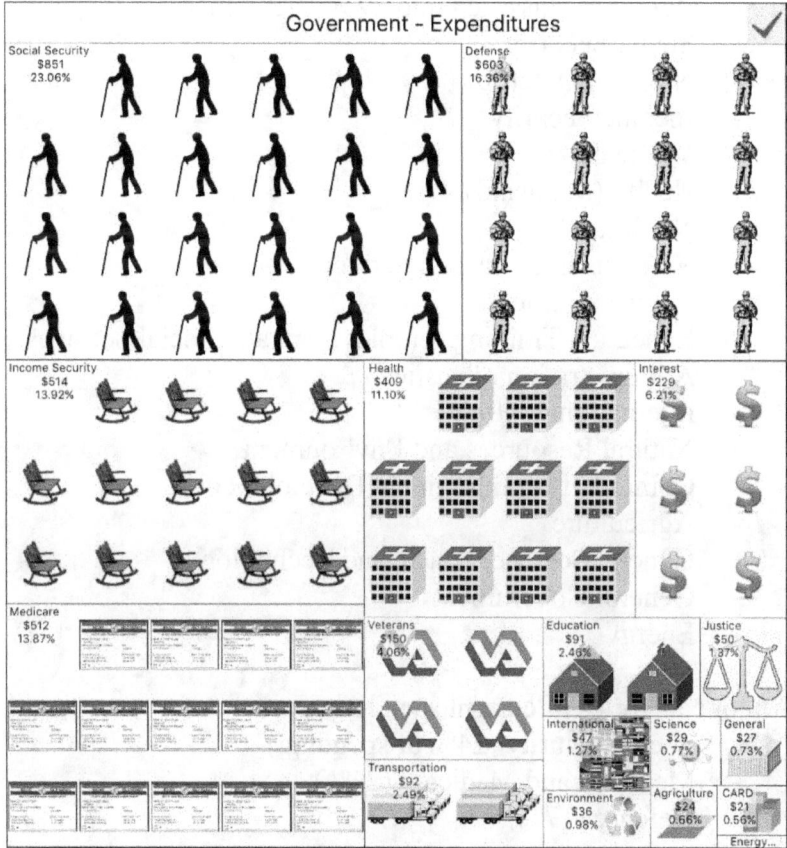

Figure 5. The Expenditures window

The budget determines how the federal government's money will be spent. The budget of the U.S. Government typically begins as the President's proposal to the U.S. Congress. The proposal recommends funding levels for the next fiscal year, which begins on October 1.

Congress is required by law to pass appropriations annually and submit funding bills, passed by the Senate and the House of Representatives, to the President for signature.

The U.S. government usually spends more money than it takes in.

Expenditures are classified into 17 budget items:
- Social Security
- National Defense
- Income Security
- Medicare
- Health (Medicaid)
- Net Interest
- Veterans Benefits and Services
- Transportation
- Education Training, Employment and Social Services
- Administration of Justice
- International Affairs
- Natural Resources and Environment
- Community and Regional Development
- Agriculture
- General Science, Space, and Technology
- General Government
- Energy

Major categories of current spending are:
- Social Security (24% of spending)
- Medicare and Medicaid (24%)
- Defense (17%)

Some expenditures are subject to mandatory spending. Some examples are:
- Social Security
- Medicare
- Income Security
- Health (Medicaid)

Expenditure beyond the mandatory minimums is called discretionary spending. Some discretionary expenditures are:
- Transportation
- International Affairs
- Science, Space and Technology

In recent years the expenditure with the most discretionary spending has been Defense.

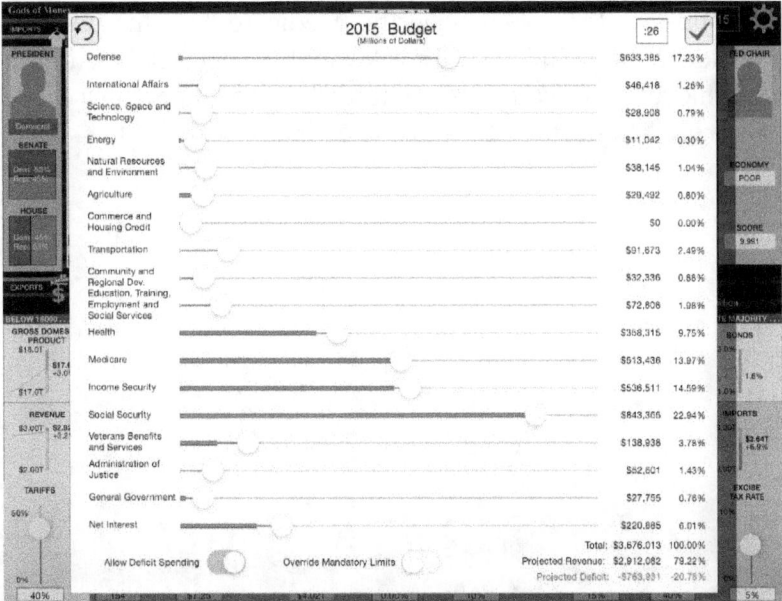

Figure 6. The Budget interface

The Budget window appears every January. The Budget window has a slider control for each budget item. Some items have a thick green band along part of the slider. This green band represents the **mandatory minimum** that must be spent on the item. In Watch mode, you can see how the White House and Congress distributed government money. In Active mode you set the amount to spend on each item by moving the slider.

When the Budget window appears in Active mode, two switches at the bottom of the window can be used to (a) allow deficit spending and (b) override mandatory limits.

Deficit spending allows the government to spend more money than it takes in, which is usually the case. When the **Allow Deficit Spending** switch is set to Off, budget items cannot be set to more that 100% of income. The **Allow Deficit Spending** switch is on by default.

The **Override Mandatory Limits** switch allows you to set budget amounts that are lower than the federally mandated minimum for some items. Setting the switch to On allows you to spend less for Social Security, Medicare, etc. In actuality, overriding the mandatory limits would be extremely difficult to achieve and would be politically very unpopular. The **Override Mandatory Limits** switch is off by default.

6. Deficit & Debt

The U.S. government raises money every year primarily by collecting taxes. The government spends money every year according to its budget. However, the government usually spends more than it receives. The resulting shortfall is called the "budget deficit."

On rare occasions, the U.S. government receives more money than it spends. This results in a "budget surplus."

The government makes up for the shortfall by borrowing money. The government typically borrows money by issuing bonds. Bonds are financial instruments people buy to receive interest payments. Bonds usually pay low interest rates. U.S. bonds are considered very safe; that is, bond investors will very likely get all their investment back in addition to interest payments.

Who buys U.S. bonds?
- Individual investors
- Corporations
- Foreign countries

The total amount of money that the U.S. government owes to creditors is called the "Federal Debt." The federal debt is sometimes referred to as the "national debt." The larger the federal debt, the more U.S. government money must be spent to pay interest.

Should the federal debt be paid off?
- Some experts say that the federal debt is too large and should be paid down.
- Other experts say that the federal debt is necessary for economic growth.

Some politicians advocate a "balanced budget" to stop increasing the federal debt. A "balanced budget amendment" would become a permanent change to the U.S. constitution.

7. Federal Reserve

The Federal Reserve System is the central banking system of the United States. Prior to the creation of the Federal Reserve:
- Markets were often unstable
    - Stock prices fluctuated
    - Real estate prices fluctuated
- People had little faith in the banking system
    - Banks sometimes failed, and many account holders lost all their money

The Federal Reserve was created by the U.S. Congress in 1913. The Federal Reserve is often called "The Fed." The Fed is an independent entity, but it is subject to oversight by Congress.

The Fed's decisions do not have to be approved by the President or anyone else in government. Congress periodically reviews the Fed's activities.

The Fed is headed by the Board of Governors of the Federal Reserve. The Board of Governors consists of 7 people appointed by the President and each member must be confirmed by the Senate. The Board is led by the Chairman.

There are 12 regional Federal Reserve Banks around the country:
- Boston
- New York
- Chicago
- St. Louis
- Philadelphia
- Cleveland
- Minneapolis
- Kansas City
- Richmond
- Atlanta
- Dallas
- San Francisco

The Fed's mandate is to promote:
- Sustainable growth
- High levels of employment
- Stability of prices
- Long-term interest rates

The Fed serves as:
- The bankers' bank
- The government's bank
- The regulator of financial institutions
- The nation's money manager

The Fed also includes the Federal Open Market Committee, better known as the FOMC.

The Fed has three main tools for influencing the economy:
- The Federal Funds Target Rate
- The Banks Reserve Requirement
- The Fed balance sheet

The Federal Funds Target Rate is the interest rate at which banks borrow reserves from each other. The FOMC sets the Federal Funds Target Rate. The Federal Funds Target Rate influences the cost of borrowing and lending money throughout the U.S. economy:
- Home loans
- Auto loans
- Personal loans
- Credit card interest rates

When the Fed changes the Federal Funds Target Rate:
- Lowering the rate means the Fed is putting more money into the economy to encourage growth.
    - A lower rate makes it cheaper to buy a house or a car, which encourages spending.
- Raising the rate means the Fed is slowing the economy to counteract or prevent inflation.
    - A higher rate makes it more expensive to buy a house or a car, which discourages spending.

The Federal Reserve also sets Bank Reserve Requirements. The bank reserve requirement is the amount of cash a bank must have in reserve compared to its total assets. The reserve requirement influences how much money banks can create through loans.
- A lower reserve requirement encourages lending and economic growth.
- A higher reserve requirement discourages lending and slows economic growth.

The Fed also influences the economy by expanding or contracting its balance sheet.
- Increasing the balance sheet encourages economic growth.
- Decreasing the balance sheet slows economic growth.

The Fed tries to sustain steady economic growth.
- If the economy grows too fast, high inflation may result.
- If the economy slows too much, a recession may occur.

The Federal Reserve is the U.S.'s central bank. Every country or economic union, such as the European Union, has a central bank. Some examples are:
- European Central Bank
- Bank of England
- Bank of Japan

8. Gold Standard

There are two types of money systems a country can have.
- Commodity money is backed by a commodity, such as gold.
- Fiat money is issued by the authority of the government.

COMMODITY MONEY
In earlier times, governments issued gold coins as money. This is called a "gold specie standard."

Later, governments adopted a "gold bullion standard:"
- Gold coins do not circulate
- The government agrees to sell gold bullion at a fixed price.
- Paper money and coins made of common metals are circulated instead of gold coins.

The U.S. was on a commodity standard for many years. From 1944 to 1971 the value of one troy ounce of gold was fixed at $35. The U.S. gold standard was completely abandoned in August 1971.

Why use gold as the commodity? Gold is:
- Rare - its scarcity means it holds its value over time
- Durable - gold does not physically degrade over time
- Divisible - gold can be melted and cast into smaller pieces
- Fungible - "gold is gold is gold;" one ounce of pure gold is the same as any other ounce of pure gold, regardless of where it is or when it was mined
- Easily identified - solid gold is easily identified by its characteristics:
    o Color
    o Density
    o Malleability (or "bendability" - pure gold is quite soft)

Commodity money has several advantages:
- Commodity money protects its users from high inflation and hyperinflation.
- Commodity money provides fixed international exchange rates
- Commodity money restricts a government using deficit spending

Commodity money has several disadvantages:
- Commodity money prevents a government's central bank from expanding the money supply to stimulate the economy.
- Commodity money may limit economic growth.
- The money supply would essentially be determined by the rate of gold production.

FIAT MONEY
In modern times, all countries use fiat money. Fiat money has one main advantage over commodity money:
- Fiat money allows expansion of the money supply which can be used to
    - Stimulate the economy
    - Rapidly raise money in times of crisis:
        - War
        - Recession
        - Depression

Fiat money also has several disadvantages:
- Fiat money can lead to high inflation and hyperinflation
- Fiat money is not backed by a physical commodity

Some people advocate the U.S. going back to commodity money.

9. Employment Tools

The federal government has two additional tools which impact employment and production: work visas and minimum wage.

WORK VISAS
Workers from foreign countries need visas to work in the U.S. By law, no more than 65,000 foreign nationals can be issued work visas each year. Many visas are valid for 3 to 6 years. In 1990, fewer than 1,000 H-1B visas were issued. Currently about 162,000 foreign workers hold H-1B visas.

Raising the number of work visas usually increases domestic production, and therefore raises the gross domestic product. Many high-tech corporations want more work visas so they can fill job openings. However, raising the number of work visas is politically unpopular, as it is seen as giving American jobs to lower-paid foreign nationals. Critics say corporations just want to lower their costs by hiring less expensive foreign workers.

There are different kinds of work visas. H-1B visas are granted to foreigners whose "specialty occupations" typically require a college degree or some other "extraordinary ability." Raising the number of work visas allowed per year may increase domestic production, but is politically unpopular. The value for work visas in *Gods of Money* represents the total number of H-1B work visas.

MINIMUM WAGE
Minimum wage is the lowest amount that an employer can pay a worker for one hour of labor. Many states and some cities have a minimum wage that is higher than the federal minimum wage. Cities such as San Francisco, Seattle, and Los Angeles will soon raise their minimum wages to about double the federal minimum wage. The minimum wage varies greatly from country to country: as of 2011, in Australia the minimum wage was $15.75 (in U.S. dollars); in the U.S, $7.25; in

Mexico, $0.58. Some countries such as Switzerland have no minimum wage.

The minimum wage is designed to prevent exploitation of workers. However, most economists believe a minimum wage makes production less efficient and increases unemployment. A higher minimum wage makes labor more expensive for the employer, who must adjust for the greater expenses by raising prices or letting employees go. One study found that raising the minimum wage 10% lowers low-skill employment by 2% to 4%. Because a higher minimum wage can induce employers to raise their prices, raising wages can lead to inflation. Some experts think a higher minimum wage stimulates the economy, but only slightly.

10. Active Mode

Gods of Money allows you to try your hand at manipulating the economy. Starting or changing to Active mode enables the controls which you can use to influence the economy.

The economic model used by *Gods of Money* is based on more than 100,000 patterns as determined by machine learning algorithms examining over 50 years of economic data. The patterns are updated quarterly as new economic data is released by the U.S.

No economic model is perfect. The results given by *Gods of Money* simulations can and will vary from actual economic behaviors. During a simulation, many events are triggered randomly, so even if you repeat your actions on otherwise identical sessions, the outcome can and will vary. Consequently, *Gods of Money* is best used in the context of an educational aid.

To start a session in Active mode:
- On the main menu, tap **Start** Gods of Money.
- Tap **Start** a new simulation.
- Select a Start Date and End Date.
- Tap **Start**.

The historical economic data will be loaded into the simulator for the start date.

To change a session from Watch mode to Active mode:
- In the Viewport, tap the "eye" icon near the upper right.
- When converting from Watch mode to Active mode, there is no end date.

In Active mode the controls become active. The political party of the President and the party make-up of the Senate and House of Representatives are shown to illustrate that when the economy is doing well, the party in office tends to remain in office; when the economy is not doing well, the party in office tends to get voted out.

HOW TO PLAY
When running in Active mode, monitor the economy and take actions as indicated. The gross domestic product and overall strength should be steadily increasing; inflation should be low but above zero; and unemployment should be about 5%.

When GDP and overall strength are decreasing, inflation is high, or unemployment is high, the economy may be slowing. When the indicators show the economy slowing, take action to stimulate the economy:
- Lower the Federal Funds Target Rate
- Increase the Assets & Liabilities
- Reduce the Reserve Requirements

When the economy may be growing too fast, take action to slow the economy:
- Raise the Federal Funds Target Rate
- Decrease the Assets & Liabilities
- Increase the Reserve Requirements

After you change one of the controls, several months of game time may pass before you see an impact on the economy. Experiment with adjusting the budget and taxes as well. The *Gods of Money* Guide can help you decide what actions to take. Turn on the guide under Settings (see Chapter 1.)

HOW TO WIN *Gods of Money*
It is possible to manipulate the economy such that the federal government can provide services without collecting taxes. When the economy has reached a state where it has a large federal surplus, the income from investing the surplus could provide all federal government services without the need for any federal taxes. When this condition occurs over the course of a year, the simulation stops and you are rewarded with the highest grade of A+.

To win a *Gods of Money* simulation:
- When starting, set No End Date
- Maintain or increase revenue
- Greatly reduce expenditures

You will soon see a budget surplus, followed by a reduction in the federal debt. Year after year the red box representing the federal debt will get smaller and smaller. Eventually, the federal debt will be paid off and you will have a federal surplus. The federal surplus will be represented by a green box behind the government box. It may take many years of game time to achieve a sufficiently large federal surplus. But eventually, the federal surplus will grow to a large size. Assuming it will generate income at about the rate of 10-year treasury bonds ("Bonds" in the dashboard), the surplus will at some point be large enough to provide enough income to pay for all federal services on its own. When that happens, there will be no need for federal taxes.

Appendix I: Recommended Reading

The Black Swan, Nassim Nicholas Taleb (2008)

Economic Indicators for Dummies, Michael Griffis (2011)

Economics for Dummies, Sean Masaki Flynn (2011)

Economics in One Lesson, Henry Hazlitt (2010)

End the Fed, Ron Paul (2010)

The Forgotten Depression: 1921: The Crash That Cured Itself, James Grant (2014)

The Great Deformation, David Stockman (2013)

Lords of Finance, Liaquat Ahamed (2010)

Money: The Unauthorized Biography, Felix Martin (2013)

Appendix II. Economic Data Resources

Federal Reserve Bank of St. Louis - Economic Research
    fred.stlouisfed.org

Office of Management and Budget - Historical Tables
    www.whitehouse.gov/omb/budget/Historicals

Bureau of Economic Analysis
    www.bea.gov

U.S. Department of Labor
    www.dol.gov

Federal Reserve System
    www.federalreserve.gov

Visual History of the Federal Reserve
    www.financialGraphart.com/history_of_fed_free.pdf

National Debt Clock
    usdebtclock.org

Wikipedia
    en.wikipedia.org

Index

accommodation 5, 18
active mode ..... v, 2, 3, 4, 10, 13, 14, 27, 39
agriculture 5, 6, 18, 26
alcohol 13
ammunition 13
arts 5, 18
assets & liabilities 11
Australia 11, 37
Auto loans 32
balance sheet 11, 32, 33
bank reserve 11, 12, 33
Board of Governors 31
bonds 29, 41
bubble 9
budget 5, 6, 8, 14, 25, 26, 27, 28, 29, 40, 45
budget deficit 8, 29
budget surplus 29, 40
bullion standard 35
businesses 1, 3, 4, 19
capital 4
central bank 11, 31, 33, 36
chair 4
commodity money 36
community 6, 26
Congress .... v, 1, 2, 11, 24, 25, 27, 31
construction 5, 18
control panel 2, 5, 10
corporate income tax 12
credit card 32
currency 12
dashboard 7, 41
defense 6, 26, 27
discretionary 26, 27
dollar strength 10
Dow Jones Industrial Average 9
education training 6, 26
educational services 5, 18
employment 32, 37, 38
energy 10
entertainment 5, 18
entrepreneurial ability 7
environment 2
exchange rate 36
excise tax 13
expenditures 8, 14, 26, 40
exports 10
extraordinary ability 37
Fed 11, 31, 32, 33, 43

federal debt 8, 29, 40
federal funds effective rate 9
federal funds target rate 11, 32
Federal Open Market Committee .32
Federal Reserve ....iii, v, 1, 2, 4, 11, 31, 33, 45
federal surplus 8, 40, 41
fiat money 12, 36
finance 5, 7, 18, 43
fishing 5, 18
FOMC 32
food services 5, 18
forestry 5, 18
fungible 35
gasoline 13, 24
GDP 5, 7, 13, 17, 18, 19
gear 3
general government 6, 26
general science 6, 26
Gods of Money ....i, iii, v, 1, 2, 13, 14, 37, 39, 40
godsofmoney.com v
gold 9, 12, 35, 36
gold standard 12, 35
government ..1, 3, 4, 5, 6, 8, 12, 14, 17, 18, 23, 24, 26, 27, 29, 31, 35, 36, 37, 40, 41
grade 2, 14, 40
gross domestic product 37
guide 2, 3, 14
H-1B 11, 37
health 5, 7, 18
health care 5, 7, 18
high grades 15
Home loans 32
House of Representatives 4, 25, 39
households 1, 4, 7, 8, 14, 21, 22
hunting 5, 18
hyperinflation 9, 12, 36
imports 10
income inequality 22
income security 6, 26
individual income tax 6
industrial production 8
inflation 9, 11, 12, 32, 33, 36, 38
information .... v, 2, 4, 14
insurance 5, 6, 18
interest 1, 6, 7, 9, 11, 24, 29, 32
international affairs 6, 26
justice 6, 26

labor 4, 11, 37, 38
leasing 5, 18
Los Angeles 37
machine learning............................39
macroeconomics ....v, 1
mandatory 6, 26, 27, 28
manufacturing 8
Medicaid 6, 26
Medicare 4, 6, 24, 26, 28
Mexico 11, 38
minimum wage 11, 37, 38
mining 8
money scale......................................4
natural Resources.......................6, 26
news crawl 4
oil 10
other services 5, 18
passive income 23
payroll taxes 24
personal income 12, 21, 23
president..4
product market 4
profits...7, 24
real estate 5, 18
recreation 5, 18
rent 5, 7, 18, 24
rental 5, 18, 24
rents..7
resource market...............................7
retirement taxes.........................6, 23
revenue5, 6, 8, 10, 12, 13, 14, 23, 24, 40
San Antonio 18
San Francisco 31, 37
Seattle...37
Senate.............................4, 25, 31, 39

services..4, 5, 7, 9, 10, 17, 18, 40, 41
settings 3, 14
shortfall 8, 29
Siri..13
social assistance 5, 18
social insurance..............................23
Social Security 4, 5, 24, 26, 28
space...6, 26
specialty occupations 37
specie standard..............................35
standard of living 1, 2, 15, 18, 19
stocks 9
Switzerland 11, 38
tariffs..24
taxes4, 5, 6, 10, 12, 13, 23, 24, 29, 40, 41
technology.................................6, 26
tips..14
tobacco 13
Toyota 18
transportation and warehousing 5, 18
troy ounce 9, 35
U.S. economy..................v, 1, 2, 32
unemployment 8, 11, 38
utilities 8
value added tax 24
VAT 24
veterans 6, 26
viewport 2, 3, 4, 39
wages 7, 23, 37, 38
watch mode 3, 4, 10, 14, 27, 39
West Texas Intermediate Crude....10
White House ....v, 1, 2, 27
wholesale trade 5, 18
work visas 11, 37

www.ingramcontent.com/pod-product-compliance
Lightning Source LLC
Chambersburg PA
CBHW070408190526
45169CB00003B/1171